Oh,

We Should Have Told You

By Sharon Clark Rowlands

A Lulu publication

CONTENTS

POEMS

FORWARD

We've all had the experience - something happens that grabs our attention and then seems to take on a life of its own. *My attention was grabbed when two days in a row two different sales clerks said to me " Oh, we should have told you."*

The next thing I knew I was flipping through a personal Journal that I had kept during several years of my Spiritual Journey, picking out stories of personal experiences and "messages from someone outside of myself" and then adding intuitively suggested subtitles to these stories and messages. "Oh, we should have told you" was transforming itself into this book.

Even though I have lived these experiences and have "heard the messages", I continue to gain wisdom and comfort each time I read them. I trust that by reading the pages of this book, you will be stimulated to reflect upon and to gain insights into your own experiences and that you will be provided with inspiration and comfort as you navigate your own Spiritual Journey.

- *Sharon Clark Rowlands, March 2009*

INTRODUCTION

I was working away at my computer when suddenly the monitor screen went blank. Almost simultaneously there was a huge bang, like a transformer had blown outside my apartment building. Seconds later the monitor screen clicked back on.

The next day I was talking with a neighbor who said that his monitor screen had not shut off, possibly because he had a heavy-duty surge protector. So I headed off to the computer shop to upgrade my surge protector.

I came home to find that neither my computer monitor nor my telephone answering machine would work when connected to this new surge protector. So I head back to the computer store to explain the situation to the clerk who says, "Oh, we should have told you that you need to hook things up in a certain sequence."

I then say that I also need some compressed air to clean my computer. The clerk says we have this new improved brand that has no chemicals and so is much more environmentally friendly and also eliminates the danger of getting chemicals into your computer. The drawback is that it's about three times more expensive. I decide that in the interest of the environment and of my computer, I will go for the improved brand.

I get home, insert a canister into the casing and start spraying my computer. In about 10 seconds the canister is empty. Thinking that maybe the canister was defective, I insert the second canister. Same thing. Ten seconds of spraying and the canister is empty.

I go back to the store and say that I have a problem with this. The clerk (a different clerk from the previous day) says "Oh, we should have told you that you need to spray in short little bursts, not in one continuous spray".

So now I'm sitting here wondering - what is the significance of me getting the message of "Oh we should have told you" two days in a row - especially since the 2nd clerk didn't ask whether I had sprayed continuously or in spurts.

And part of me is screaming:

"What else is there that YOU SHOULD HAVE TOLD ME?"

WE SHOULD HAVE TOLD YOU

*That Your Spiritual Journey Will Frequently Begin With a
Crisis of Some Kind*

I sat in stunned disbelief. In my entire working life, I had never been fired. Yet here I was, sitting in the administrative office of my newly acquired Group Home job, being informed that my services were no longer required. Although the administration used politically correct phrases to assure me that I was not being "fired", to me, being told that my services were no longer required equated to being fired.

As I was adjusting to this bit of news, I was hit by another realization. The lease on my car was expiring the next month. It had been my intention to purchase the car for the Buyout amount of $4000. I had been debating whether to pay all $4000 in cash, to finance all of it, or to finance part of it. Suddenly I thought, "Oh my God, with no job, I may not be able to finance any of it". Paying all cash would leave me with $4000 less in my bank account at a time when I would have no source of income.

I made my way home where I sat thinking: I can't believe that I am sitting here, a few months short of my 50th birthday, with no job and facing the possibility of having no car.

WE SHOULD HAVE TOLD YOU

That Synchronicities Will Appear # 1

As I sat contemplating the loss of my job and the possible loss of my car, I had a phone call from a friend, who was deeply into what my other friends and I called "mystical / spiritual stuff." When I told this friend that I didn't know what I was going to do, now that my services were no longer required at the Group Home job, my friend asked what I would like to do. I heard myself saying that what I would really like to do is to sit by the ocean and listen to the waves and the seagulls. Rather than saying "get real" or "what are you really going to do", this friend asked how I was going to make that happen. I laughed and said "Yea, like in this lifetime I'm meant to live on the ocean!"

It seemed that I had just hung up from this call when another friend phoned. This friend had recently moved to a house on the beach on a nearby Island. As I was telling her about my previous phone call, my friend said that the cabin down the beach from her house was for rent.

What was going on here? In the span of a few hours, I had lost my job, tapped into a desire to spend time with the waves and the seagulls and now I was being told of a cabin on the beach for rent.

WE SHOULD HAVE TOLD YOU

That the Early Synchronicities Will Cause Confusion # 1

I decided to check out the cabin. It was perfect. Yes it was rustic, the windows were single glaze and the refrigerator was of rounded corners vintage. But it was fronted by 20 feet of floor to ceiling windows and the deck was so close to the water that the waves lapped right up to the deck's edge, even under it during storms.

As I stood on that deck, breathed in the salt air and listened to the waves and the seagulls, I knew that I needed to spend time at that cabin. But what a life-changing decision that would be! In order to commit to this rental, I would need to sell my home. This idea frightened me. For years owning my own home had provided the bulk of my security. Could I give up that security and return to renting?

WE SHOULD HAVE TOLD YOU

That the Early Synchronicities Will Cause Confusion # 2

There was also the issue of whether I should trust this synchronicity of events. After my second marriage dissolved, I had spent time living somewhat precariously both financially and emotionally all the while believing that when I needed a conventional job, a certain friend would be instrumental in helping me.

When the day came that I needed that job, my friend advised that he knew of an agency that was looking for childcare workers. I applied and was offered a job. When I later learned that I had been offered the job after someone else had declined, I took that as a sign that I was where I was supposed to be.

Yet a few months later, I was sitting in the administrative office being told that my services were no longer required.

I had trusted that that job was where I was supposed to be.

And I had been proven wrong.

WE SHOULD HAVE TOLD YOU

That the Early Synchronicities Will Cause Confusion # 3

But back came the memory of standing on that deck and the knowing that I needed to be there. Also came thoughts of how I had tried to do things in ways that seemed to work for other people. I had gone to school, gone to work, paid my bills, raised my children, yet here I sat with no job, no relationship, not much savings in the bank. Maybe there was something I was missing or that I didn't understand. I found myself writing a poem:

OTHER ACCOUNTS

I've tried to do what I've been told I should
Tried to be diligent, responsible and good.
I've raised my children and paid my bills,
Now I'm wondering about life's other thrills.

I know that I can do the old way no more
My children are grown, seems that is a door
To freedom and fear mixed in equal amounts
A time to focus on other accounts.

On account of I'm confused, don't know who I am
Don't know what I want or how to be all that I can.
On account of I know I can't find out the old way,
So I'm off to find me is all I can say.

WE SHOULD HAVE TOLD YOU

That Outer Change Will Bring Inner Change # 1

I decided to rent the cabin. Once there, my newfound freedom from my previous responsibilities felt strange and somewhat confusing. No more alarm clock, no more job to show up to, very little housework, just one linoleum floor that needed occasional sweeping.

Yes there were challenges, like the time that I waited three days for the sun to thaw the hose that connected the cabin taps to the water main on the road. But each morning as I rounded the corner from the bedroom to the living room, the view from the floor to ceiling windows took my breath away.

And there was lots of animal life. Seagulls and crows visited on the deck, sea otter and seals swam in the bay, deer wandered down to drink at the nearby stream. I felt like a kid in a playhouse.

WE SHOULD HAVE TOLD YOU

That Outer Change Will Bring Inner Change # 2

There was time for romance, the demise of one of which was to have a dramatic effect on my life. A friend and I were discussing what we considered to be appropriate behavior. I was defending my right to excuse myself from dinners being attended by people whose conversations I did not enjoy.

My friend asked if I thought that it was OK for people to choose not to listen to each other talk about certain issues. I said "Yes I do. I think that we each have a responsibility to take care of ourselves. And one of those ways we do this is by choosing what we allow ourselves to be exposed to." My friend then said "OK, I don't want to listen to you talk about that man you used to be involved with."

That conversation changed my life. The friend who made this announcement was the person with whom I spoke the most frequently at that time. And now she was refusing to listen to me talk about the breakup of my romantic relationship.

When I no longer had the luxury of relating my tale of woe about what this man had done or not done, I was forced to find other things to talk about which meant other things to think about.

WE SHOULD HAVE TOLD YOU

That Outer Change Will Bring Inner Change # 3

I began thinking of things that I had been too busy and perhaps too fearful to think about before. I thought about how I, and others, had always considered me to be optimistic, yet now that I was becoming more conscious of my thoughts, I saw how my mind frequently went first to the possibility of the "worst case scenario". I think that previously I had appeared optimistic to myself and to others, because I had just skipped over these worse case scenario thoughts, ignoring that I was even having them.

During my newfound "thinking time" my daughter graduated from university and I thought of the parents of a friend of my daughter, who many times during my years as a single parent, had taken my daughter to their summer place for much of her school summer holidays. Only now was I realizing what a major factor that had been in both my life and my daughter's life. I sat down and wrote a Thank You letter to these friends.

That one Thank You letter led me to remember many other people who had gone out of their way to help my children and me. It also led me to the realization that for many years I had been so focused on the people who had not helped me, that I had not fully appreciated the many people who had helped me.

Then the questions started. Had my life in fact been rather easy and I had been an ungrateful complainer? Would I come to realize that I had been responsible for missing joy and happiness that I could have had?

In an attempt to answer these questions, I read possibly every Self Help and Personal Growth book that had ever been written.

WE SHOULD HAVE TOLD YOU

That Your Friends Will Begin to Consider You Weird #1

I had never been much of a television watcher and now between sky gazing, watching the wildlife, chopping firewood and driving to a nearby marina for laundry and groceries, I seldom even followed the news.

Friends chastised me saying that it was important that we all know what is going in the world.

When I told them that I sometimes watched Royal Canadian Air Farce or This Hour has 22 Minutes, they expressed concern that I wasn't getting the facts.

I countered that maybe I was.

WE SHOULD HAVE TOLD YOU

That You Will Tend to Doubt the Early Synchronicities

As the cabin was not really winterized I would need a lot of firewood for the stove that provided the main source of heating. So I ordered the firewood and headed out to the hardware store to buy myself an axe.

Upon finding the axe aisle my eyes were immediately drawn to a pretty axe with a red head and a yellow handle.

But noticing that there seemed to be a surprisingly large selection of axes I spent some time trying to figure out why there were so many.

Deciding that the axes came in different handle lengths and various axe head weights I tried several until I felt I knew which handle length and head weight was right for me.

Then I went back to the pretty one that had first caught my eye.

Yup perfect handle length and head weight for me.

WE SHOULD HAVE TOLD YOU

That Your Body Will Help You Learn About Yourself # 1

I had developed bursitis in my right shoulder and could barely move my arm away from my body. Though the pain was bearable, the inconvenience was enormous. Heating the cabin required two or three large armloads of firewood each day. Having only one functioning arm meant carrying in the firewood one piece at a time which stretched a 5 minute job into almost an hour as part of the process was putting down the one piece of firewood, to open the heavy sliding glass door, which had to be closed between each trip in order to prevent having rodents as roommates.

A woman I had recently met had come by for a visit. As she was preparing to leave, I was thinking that the logical thing to do was to ask her to carry in an armload of firewood for me. My conditioning said, "But you have just met her, but she may not want to carry in firewood, but she's not really dressed for the job, etc. "

When I finally asked her if she would carry in the firewood, she said of course. Later I thought, no wonder my life has tended to be difficult at times. I have been operating under the illusion that I have to do everything for myself.

WE SHOULD HAVE TOLD YOU

*That Spiritual Teachings Will Seem Confusing
in the Beginning # 1*

My reading of Self Help and Personal Growth books evolved into me reading books about Spirituality. This led me to deeper thinking and also to some confusion about what appeared to be discrepancies.

On the one hand during my Practicum for the Group Home job, I had spent time at each of the three houses that the Agency operated. I had then "decided on" the house I wanted and I had gotten a position at that house. So weren't these Spiritual books saying that that meant I had been putting out my Intention and seeing it manifest? So how come I wasn't still at that job?

On the other hand, I remembered the time that I had looked at the yellow and green tile counter top in my kitchen and knew that it had to go. Having neither a plan nor a budget, I just started the dismantling. Then one of my Real Estate clients was moving from a house that had been bought by a developer and the client's house was to be destroyed. The updated kitchen cabinets from the client's house had fitted into my kitchen like they had been custom made.

WE SHOULD HAVE TOLD YOU

*That Spiritual Teachings Will Seem Confusing
in the Beginning # 2*

When I was reading about Creative Visualization, I gasped as I remembered the day that I had decided to teach myself to ride a bicycle. A friend of my brother's had left his bike leaning against our barn. A perfect opportunity.

I had known that in order to gain my balance, it would be necessary to attain a certain amount of speed. The road in front of my parents' farm was paved, and went gently downhill from our driveway. I figured that should take care of gaining the speed, but what to do about the fact that I didn't know how to make the bike stop? I had decided that I would pull into the driveway of a neighboring farm just before the road went into a steep turn. I figured that when I stopped pedaling, the bike would coast to a standstill.

I got up on the bike and pushed off. After a couple of wiggles, the bike and I were upright. Soon however, I realized, that the bike was picking up speed much faster than I had anticipated. I had a fleeting moment of panic and then somehow I knew to keep picturing the bike and myself safely pulling into that driveway and coasting to a stop just as I had envisioned. So had I actually "known" about Creative Visualization as a kid?

WE SHOULD HAVE TOLD YOU

That Your Body Holds Memories # 1

As I read about Emotional Freedom Technique (EFT) I thought about the first time that I had flown into Mexico.

As the plane was descending, I had suddenly had a horrendous headache, which was surprising as I am not generally prone to headaches. But across my brow there was a line like a headband of points that felt like they might burst. The pressure/pain was one of the most intense I have ever felt.

I remembered how I had leaned forward and instinctively tapped along my brow. At the time I had no idea why that suggestion came to me.

Now I'm wondering if my body had some memory that prompted me to tap along my brow.

WE SHOULD HAVE TOLD YOU

That You Will Come to Feel That You Are Having Conversations With Someone Outside of Yourself # 1

I had now spent enough time by myself, to have allowed my mental dialogue to quiet to the point where I could actually hear both sides of this dialogue. It was like one part of my mind was talking to another part of my mind.

Slowly, this listening to both sides of my mental dialogue and my Journal writing started to blend. I would write a question, like "What am I to do next?" and then write the response that came to me. Many of these responses surprised me.

Some people might question where these responses were coming from.

I chose not to question, just to listen and to write.

Some of these "conversations" went like this:

I feel like I'm reaching deep inside of myself for something.

You are reaching inside of yourself for Clarity.

Clarity about what?

About yourself.

What about myself?

That you have forgotten how to be happy and joyful and trusting.

How do I get that back?

By remembering to laugh and to play. And to clean up your life.

What does that mean to clean up my life?

It means that you are carrying pain and anger in your body. That needs to be released.

How do I do that?

You know how to do that. Move around, cry, shout, laugh.

WE SHOULD HAVE TOLD YOU

That You Will Come to Feel That You Are Having Conversations With Someone Outside of Yourself # 2

What is the significance of the double numbers (11:11 and 12:12) that I seem to see frequently on the clock and that I feel I respond to?

They are reminders for you

Reminders of what?

Reminders that you are connected to us.

That we are here for you, and

That we have messages for you.

Can you tell me what the messages are?

That we love you.

That we want what is best for you and

That we are offering you encouragement.

Also to remind you to listen for the Messages.

And to ask for the messages.

WE SHOULD HAVE TOLD YOU

That You Will Come to Feel That You Are Having Conversations With Someone Outside of Yourself # 3

I am finding this whole process rather confusing.

We are pleased that you are beginning to learn to sit through your confusion, without rushing off to look for answers from others. Yes, you are still searching for answers in books, but in books we can guide you to certain ideas. With other people, their script may interfere with yours and you may not be able to discern that in a way that is healthy.

Why am I thinking of releasing the computer that my friend gave me, when I have never even hooked it up?

Because it is electronic.

So ?

It is important at the moment, for you to have direct hands on experience, like writing with a pen as it is in the physical writing that we are best able to communicate with you.

WE SHOULD HAVE TOLD YOU

That You Will Come to Feel That You Are Having
Conversations With Someone Outside of Yourself # 4

Am I making progress here?

Yes, you are making progress. We know that you are
reviewing past mistakes, but those were lessons. They were
painful in many ways, but they were lessons that you chose, or
that you needed. It is true that you have tended to create some
precarious situations both financially and emotionally. It is also
true that these experiences are leading you deeper into yourself.
You are letting go of Self Pity. You are learning to release
mental anguish and pretense. You are learning to release
judgement or at least to be conscious of it when you have it.
These are major steps.

These major steps resulted in me beginning to feel
uncomfortable in social situations. Shortly after arriving at
some gathering, I would feel like going home. As it was winter
time I told myself that if I left the cabin fire unattended for too
long a period of time, that the cabin temperature would be
unbearable upon my return. But I knew that it was more than
that. I had dropped many of my defenses and my pretenses
and I had not yet put anything in their place. I felt like a
crustacean that had shed its shell.

WE SHOULD HAVE TOLD YOU

That Your Spiritual Journey Will Frequently Return to a Crisis of Some Kind

I learned that the investment in which I had placed the proceeds from the sale of my home had failed and that I therefore, basically had no money.

What am I to do about supporting myself financially?

Focus on remembering your dreams, while also taking action steps. Do something if you are seriously playing this game.

This Game?

This Game of Life.

I have been reading about Putting out Intentions. Should I be doing this?

If you choose.

OK I will put out an Intention that I will receive some cash.

You can put out that Intention, but do you believe it?

I believe, that since I lost some money in a bad investment, that there's some of "my cash" out there, so it would be Ok for me to ask for it back.

What if there was not any of "your cash" out there, would it still be OK to ask for some? You find that question more difficult do you not?

Overcoming a sense of not deserving is really hard.

There is enough for everyone, so you can receive everything you want.

There are resources out there that you are not even aware of, so maintain faith.

Set your Intention on creating a life that incorporates all of the things that are important to you.

At the same time, intend that you will allow as much of your old stuff as possible to clear.

This is how you create a balanced life.

WE SHOULD HAVE TOLD YOU

That You Will Come to Feel That You Are Having Conversations With Someone Outside of Yourself # 5

Why do I have so much trouble coming up with the answers as to what I want?

Time and money. You tell yourself that you do not have enough of either and so you hold yourself back from even thinking about doing things or of having things. You have blocked yourself from admitting what you want. You have held yourself back from enjoying life.

How do I change this?

You start believing that you deserve to have good things happen in your life. Ask us for help. We can only help you when you ask.

Thank You that many of the things that I ask for have been working out.

But you ask for so little. We can help you even more if you ask. Many of the previous things that you have asked for and received could be considered small things by some people's standards. Yet they are miracles. And miracles are miracles. Once you begin shopping in the Store of Miracles, you are at least in the right store.

Also remain aware of situations. Attracting situations is a part of manifesting, so you do not always need to be directing the movie, especially in the early stages when you are still learning. It is true that the clearer you are, the clearer will be the situations that you attract.

WE SHOULD HAVE TOLD YOU

That You Will Come to Feel That You Are Having Conversations With Someone Outside of Yourself # 6

What part am I to play in all of this?

You need only to get clear about what it is that you want and very clear that you deserve it. Trust that you will be provided for, not necessarily taken care of, but provided for. If you desire a job, one will be provided for you.

Would a job interfere with my time with you guys?

Only if you allow it. If you set this time with us as a priority, it will be provided. Your Belief Systems are like computers. They rely on what you feed into them.

WE SHOULD HAVE TOLD YOU

That Your Spiritual Path Will Involve Goodbyes

My changed financial situation meant that it was time to say Goodbye to the Cabin which led to the following poem:

CABIN YOU'VE BEEN GOOD FOR ME

Cabin you've been good for me
You've helped me listen, you've helped me see
Things out there beyond the walls
Walls of yours and walls of mine
Walls that frame us in space and time

You were old and I was new
Together we saw each other through
Sunny days and long cold nights
Star filled skies and Northern Lights

The rainbows came and then the swan
Frequently I was awake at dawn
Eager to see what each day would bring
Thrilled to hear the little birds sing

I've really enjoyed my time with you
I laughed, I cried, I danced, I grew
I'll always remember your loving embrace
Though another home may take your place
We'll each go on to other people and things
Remembering each other whatever life brings.

WE SHOULD HAVE TOLD YOU

That Synchronicities Will Appear # 2

So I loaded up my car and drove to the ferry that would carry me back to the mainland and the next phase of my Journey, which began with a search for affordable accommodation. As the cabin had been furnished and I had envisioned staying there for several years, I had sold most of my furniture before moving. Now with limited funds and not much furniture, I considered the possibility of renting a bed-sitting room.

The next morning's Classifieds advertised such a room on the ground floor of a house. But as I stood in the windowless kitchenette, I knew that I could not live there.

During a coffee with the owner of the house she and I arranged for me to house-sit the vacant house of her deceased parents where I stayed until the house sold.

WE SHOULD HAVE TOLD YOU

That You Will Come to Feel That You Are Having
Conversations With Someone Outside of Yourself # 7

What about my present refusal to accept that finding a job will be as hard as other people are saying it will be?

It is a mirror, for you to see how people believing that the universe is unfriendly, tends to make it so for them. That is why you were given the experience of finding the Group Home job. So that you could remember that when you are clear and focused on your Intent, then it happens. At the time that you received that job, you had a Belief that it would happen, and it did.

However at that time you were still operating intellectually, you were not in touch with your emotions. Now that you are getting in touch with your emotions, you are finding things a bit more confusing because your fears are surfacing.

So what do I do now?

Now you feel your feelings. Feel your fear. Feel your sadness. Allow each feeling. Tell each feeling that it is OK for it to be there. We will help you with this. We have been waiting a long time for you to get in touch with your feelings.

WE SHOULD HAVE TOLD YOU

*That You Will Come to Feel That You Are Having
Conversations With Someone Outside of Yourself # 8*

A friend suggested someone to contact for a possible job as a Property Agent and two weeks later, I was at my new office. The job was busy, busy, busy. I reached a point, where the job was always on my mind. I would wake at night thinking about things that needed to be done or that I worried would not get done. I was not happy that this was my life.

You feel unhappy because you view the circumstances of your life and see that they are not to your liking and so you feel sad. The sadness comes from a Belief that you are unable to change these circumstances.

WE SHOULD HAVE TOLD YOU

That You Can Let Go of Your Beliefs # 1

I decided to start trusting that things at my busy job would get done on time. And they did. Sometimes before leaving the office for the day, I would sort papers into piles according to topic and jokingly say "OK Spirit organize this". Frequently returning to my desk the next morning the piles did seem less confusing than the previous afternoon.

And many times when I had difficult or sensitive material to write, in the quiet early morning as I was writing in my Journal, I would suddenly know just the phrases to use. It was as though one part of my mind was focusing on Journal writing while the other part was focusing on the work related material.

And as I went along in the job, I realized that I could have some flexibility in my work hours which confirmed what the Messages had said about a job not interfering if I put early morning time with my Journal Writing as a Priority.

There went one of my Beliefs.

WE SHOULD HAVE TOLD YOU

That You Can Stop Replaying Old Tapes in Your Mind # 1

Over the course of several months I had much more than usual contact with both my biological family as well as the biological family of my grown children's dad, due to weddings, births, deaths, and graduations. Attending these gatherings was like replaying lots of old situations and experiences, sometimes even with the original players.

What seemed to happen was that an incident or a situation would occur and I could hear myself start to play the Old Tapes of "what so and so will do next", "how that will make the other person feel", "how I will then feel" etc, etc. Hearing these Old Tapes play I could feel my discomfort upon seeing my contribution in the Old Situations.

But this time instead of repeating my part in the Old Tapes, I seemed to be able to remain silent while reminding myself that these were Old Tapes and that they did not need to be replayed. I saw myself beginning to Let Go of some of my old needs to blame and to fix.

WE SHOULD HAVE TOLD YOU

That You Can Stop Replaying Old Tapes in Your Mind # 2

My daughter was talking about possible ways to re-arrange a small two bedroom house to accommodate herself, her husband, their 4 yr. old son, their new baby and a study area for my daughter.

My daughter's final analysis basically meant rearranging and re-allocating every room in the house - and doing it over the next 4 weekends. I went into "helpful mom" mode thinking I would / could / should offer to help. But that is not what I wanted to do for the next four weekends. So, for a couple of days, I went back and forth - I don't want to give up four weekends, your daughter needs your help, I don't want to, etc.

Then my daughter and I came up with a solution which was so simple. I realized that previously, I would have stayed in "helpful mom" mode and helped for the four weekends, all the while somewhat resenting it, and quite likely feeling guilty about resenting it.

This time, I allowed myself to acknowledge what I wanted - freedom for the four weekends. And a solution presented itself that pleased both my daughter and me.

WE SHOULD HAVE TOLD YOU

That You Can Stop Replaying Old Tapes in Your Mind # 3

I had offended a friend. As we began discussing the situation, I initially tried explaining why I had done what I did (I was in the "wrong" in this particular instance). Then, apparently, once we had established that I would accept responsibility for one wrong, my friend started on a Laundry List of grievances that she had about me. I defended myself against 2 or 3 more accusations, but I had the sense that my friend would not be satisfied until I was on my knees groveling for our friendship.

Suddenly, it was like something turned over in my brain, and I heard myself saying "You know, if I thought I was as terrible as you seem to think I am, I wouldn't have anything to do with me." These words surprised me as much as they did my friend.

WE SHOULD HAVE TOLD YOU

That You Can Stop Replaying Old Tapes in Your Mind # 4

I had joined a new Discussion Group. During one session, another member and I had a rather heated disagreement about the appropriateness of her interrupting others during their sharing.

At the following session, the other group member began talking about when one person does something to push another person's buttons and I sensed that she was referring to her and my former interchange.

I started listening, wondering who she was referring to as the pusher of the buttons. I saw myself start my old tapes of: I need to defend myself, point out why I think she is wrong, etc.

Then I realized that it didn't really matter to me who she thought she was referring to or what point she was trying to make. I had already expressed my viewpoint regarding the earlier situation. My choice was to let the issue go and to be happy.

WE SHOULD HAVE TOLD YOU

That You Will Begin to Trust Synchronicity # 1

I had been wondering how to catch the shuttle bus to the airport. As I was walking to my car I realized that I had forgotten my cigarettes in my apartment. I felt nudged to go back up to the apartment to get them, as opposed to stopping at the corner store to buy another pack.

Coming back down in the elevator, I talked with a man carrying a suitcase and learned that the shuttle bus stopped at the nearby local hotel.

Aha! So that's why I had felt the nudge to return to my apartment.

WE SHOULD HAVE TOLD YOU

That Things Will Show Up Where You Least Expect Them

Having decided to buy a jogging suit, I had visited several department stores only to find that they no longer seemed to carry these suits. I wondered if I was going to have to seek out a Sporting Goods store.

Then one day I stopped at a local Thrift Shop that sells paperback books for $1 and which I tend to use essentially as a library. This particular day the shop had some clothes for sale and I saw a fuschia-colored jogging suit in my size, brand new with a price tag of $15. And that day they were having a 50% off sale. So at my "library" I got an $80 jogging suit for $7.50.

WE SHOULD HAVE TOLD YOU

That Some of Your Beliefs Will Surprise You # 1

I was wandering through London Drugs when I noticed that I had picked up 3 items, two for my grandson and one that could be used by a group that I belong to. I had not picked up anything for myself. And I realized that I do this all the time. I tend to pick up things for others rather than for myself.

Then I came to a "Candle Clearance" and my eyes lit on some beautiful pink cube candles that looked like children's building blocks and that smelled wonderfully of Peony. They were $10 reduced to $3, so I bought 2 for myself.

Later I realized that I was being shown Beliefs - "buy for others before self" and "stock up on bargains".

WE SHOULD HAVE TOLD YOU

That Some of Your Beliefs Will Surprise You # 2

My adult son had stopped by. Even though I was in my bathrobe and slippers, I walked with him to his friend's car to say goodbye. My son was embarrassed that I would step out of my apartment building and onto the sidewalk in my bathrobe - which was neck-to-ankle terry cloth. I said to him, what's the big deal? My body is covered.

Later as I was telling this story to a friend, we each realized that we might have been less comfortable wearing a bathrobe on the sidewalk in an area where more people might see us. Then we asked why do we have a Belief that it's "embarrassing or shameful" to wear a bathrobe where people may see us?

WE SHOULD HAVE TOLD YOU

That You Will Begin to Trust Synchronicity # 2

One day I walked into a new friend's apartment in a building across the street from a beach and I knew that I could very happily live in that setting. I was shown an apartment that was custom made for me. It had hardwood floors and a view that encompassed the ocean, rocks, trees, sand, flowers and mountains in the distance. Amazing!

While I gazed at the view I "heard": You are drawn to the water's edge because it is where you feel happy and free because you are not boxed in. You can see and feel the beauty of the universe, which allows your Spirit to soar. That view down the strait is a passageway – a Northwest passageway.

This reference to the direction of the passageway may have reflected the fact that I had joined a class on Native American teachings. During the classes the facilitator would beat on a drum while the class lay on the floor and went on Journeys.

At first I was able only to lie on the floor and enjoy feeling the drumbeat through my body. Then slowly I began to have glimpses of what going on a Journey was about.

My first glimpse was when we were to connect with our Animal Totem. I giggled as I saw myself walking down a path with the A&W bear. But at least I was finally Journeying, he was an animal and he did lead me to connect with a salmon and an eagle.

WE SHOULD HAVE TOLD YOU

That You Will Come to Learn When Others Are Willing to Play With You

Arriving at the local service station, I saw that the Lottery was $22,000,000. Remembering that I had two lottery tickets in my wallet, I had the fun thought that I would cash in these tickets and use the $2 winnings to buy the winning ticket for the $22,000,000.

I took my tickets to the man, saying I want to cash in these two tickets to buy the winning ticket for the $22,000,000. The man put the first ticket into the machine and said there's $1.

Then he held up the second ticket and asked "how much do you want for this one?" Still playing my original game, I said well another $1 to buy the winning ticket for the $22,000,000. And that's what I got!

Later I wondered what might have happened if I had said I wanted $100,000 or $1,000,000 for the second ticket. The man was playing the game with me, he had his hand on the machine - and I didn't see the opportunity.

WE SHOULD HAVE TOLD YOU

That There Is Balance Even in the Midst of Seeming Chaos

I live in an apartment building where the laundry room has two washers and two dryers. I had gone down to do a load of laundry. When I opened the laundry room door I saw several piles of clothes on the tables beside the machines and I could hear a dryer running. I decided to leave my load of laundry and come back later.

As I was putting my laundry on the table next to the washers, I noticed a "machine broken" sign.

Ah - one washer is broken and the clothes on that table were in the washer when it broke.

Ah - and the second washer is actually available.

Then I checked the 2 piles by the dryer.

Ah - they're each already dry. I looked closely at the dryers and I saw that only one dryer was running and the other one was empty.

So actually, in the midst of all of that chaos, there was one washer and one dryer available for my one load of laundry. That possibility had never entered my mind when I first opened the Laundry Room door. In fact I wasn't able to let the possibility in until I had decided to "put down my own load."

WE SHOULD HAVE TOLD YOU

That Some Things Will At Least Give Your Friends a Laugh

Glancing out the window of my apartment, I saw that some neighbors were setting up for a lawn sale. My eyes went to a piece of furniture. Oh I love the golden colored wood frame and the muslin cloth cushions. But what is it exactly? To satisfy my curiosity, I walked outside for a closer look.

It was a Futon sofa in two sections that could be used as either a loveseat and ottoman combination or as a bed. I loved it and it would be perfect in my little apartment.

Then the "buts" set in:

But I don't have room unless I get rid of my current sofa.

But I would need help moving the sofa out and the futon in.

But my apartment isn't clean enough to have people in to help me.

And by the time I had put my buts to rest the futon was gone.

However all was not lost, as it did give my friends an opportunity to coin the phrase "Don't fut on yourself".

WE SHOULD HAVE TOLD YOU

That Some Experiences Will Seem Weird Even to You # 1

I had gone to the beach and sat for a time on a bench taking in the natural beauty. Then I had the thought to lie down, so I stretched out on the grass in front of the bench. After I had made myself comfortable, I gazed out at the water, the mountains and the trees, and I thought "This is Heaven." Almost immediately I heard harp music !

As I was congratulating myself on how my imagination had increased, I thought "that isn't your imagination". So, I looked up and Sure Enough, behind the bench, there was a guy playing a huge harp.

Later as I was telling a neighbor about saying "This is Heaven" and then hearing the harp music, my neighbor was kind enough (or not) to point out, that it was unfortunate that I hadn't said that I felt like a millionaire.

WE SHOULD HAVE TOLD YOU

*That You Will Come to Feel That You Are Having
Conversations With Someone Outside of Yourself # 9*

Why am I hesitant to phone my office to say that I will be staying home because I am sick?

It is about your Sense of Responsibility which is tied to the work ethic – that one must be working / contributing / producing to justify one's existence, one's right to be here.

A part of you knows that you are well enough to go to the office today if you choose to force yourself. So you are facing guilt that you are taking advantage of someone, even though you know that it serves you to honor yourself by staying home.

Am I rather stuck around my work?

Yes, because you see it in contrast to the freedom that you are learning to have in the rest of your life. However the job is providing stability, grounding, and anchoring so that you can get clear.

Get clear about what?

About the things that you do not want. Once you get clear about what you do not want you can move towards what you do want. The first step is to stop forcing yourself to do things that you don't really want to do.

WE SHOULD HAVE TOLD YOU

That Some Things Are Just Too Coincidental

While I had begun to realize that my days at my current job were numbered, I hadn't reached a decision about when I might leave. Apparently Spirit had!

My son and his Japanese fiancé were awaiting my daughter's wedding in Canada before heading off to Japan. Several family members were gathered at my daughter's house. Discussion had led to the suggestion that following my daughter's wedding, family members could travel to Japan courtesy of my children's father who was an airline employee, and have my son's wedding there. While this plan excited everyone involved, I knew that if I were to be away from my desk for the required 3 consecutive weeks, that I would not be able to make myself return to face my work backlog.

As I was driving away from my daughter's house, I became aware of a vision of a train speeding along beside my car. I sensed that I was being asked if I intended to get on this train. I also sensed that I was being informed that if I did get on, that neither I nor my life would ever be the same. I spent a restless night.

The next morning I remembered that the company I was working for, asked employees to give thirty days notice when they were leaving. I counted the days until my time off for my daughter's wedding…thirty!

Then I almost burst out laughing as I realized that I already had an appointment that day, with the person to whom I would need to give my notice. It seemed preordained.

WE SHOULD HAVE TOLD YOU

That There Will Be Times When You Surprise Yourself

So I gave notice at my job and prepared for the marriages of each of my children. Ten days after my daughter married in a long white gown wedding in Canada, my son married in a Buddhist Shrine in Japan.

Standing in the Reception Line of my son's wedding, breaking every behavior protocol I had been told about how the Japanese did not like to hug, I thought "Well, then they should not have served champagne, wine and saki before the Receiving Line." What's a mother to do when she is facing the sobering experience that the next morning she will be on a plane back to Canada leaving her child to begin a new life thousands of miles away?

So I allowed my emotions to bubble to the surface and hugged each person as they came through the Receiving Line. And you know what? As I hugged, the Japanese hugged right back.

WE SHOULD HAVE TOLD YOU

That Synchronicities Will Appear # 3

A friend had suggested that she would like myself and another woman who was also following a Spiritual Path, to move into my friend's house. This felt like a chance to practice a Retreat House idea I had, so I had given notice to vacate my apartment and move to my friend's house when I returned from Japan. The third woman ended up not staying long at the house and my friend continued at her job, so we didn't get much Retreat House experience.

When it became time to move on from my friend's house, I checked out the apartment building by the beach where I had lived before. While I knew that I could envision living in that apartment building again, I wasn't so certain that I could see myself back at my previous job to pay the rent.

Then one morning I asked myself what I would really like to do. Hearing that I just wanted to lie in the sun, I e-mailed a friend who spends several winter months in Arizona. Yes, my friend would be happy to have me visit. I stayed in Arizona for eight wonderful weeks by which time my funds were getting low and it was once again decision making time.

WE SHOULD HAVE TOLD YOU

That Sometimes It Will Feel Like You Are Going in Circles # 1

I returned to my home province and accepted an offer to stay with a friend in my old neighborhood by the beach. One day as I was walking out the front door of my friend's building, the manager was putting up a Vacancy sign for a studio suite which I decided would be a perfect temporary solution.

Then my old job became available. While I had resistance to returning to the job, I also had fear about not taking it. I decided to take the job but it wasn't long before I was asking why I had chosen to do so.

You have chosen to return to this job because it is the safest place for you to embrace your next stage of growth.

If I'm choosing it then why am I also resisting it?

Because only part of you is choosing it.

I have bronchitis symptoms. What's that about?

These bronchitis symptoms are allowing for emotional clearing.

What kind of emotional clearing?

The clearing of resentment.

Resentment about what?

About the fact that you feel that others are being demanding and unreasonable, while you hold the Belief that everyone is to be reasonable and to get along.

That's true. I do hold that Belief, which reminds me of a poem that I wrote:

I ALWAYS THOUGHT THERE WAS ANOTHER WAY

I always thought there was another way
Though I tried to do what I heard you say
Walk don't run and be quiet please
Act like a lady and always be nice
Follow this year's fashions and learn to conform
Mind your manners and don't complain
Life was meant to be difficult. Don't be vain
Thinking you deserve a different lot
Than all of the others you see each day
It's best to learn to live life their way

But why I asked is everyone so glum
What would be wrong with a little fun
What if we laughed and played as we worked
What if we said oh you believe that, funny I believe this
If we're honest and kind we'll be OK
I always thought there was a different way
A way that allows us all to just be
You to be you and me to be me
Side by side we would face each new day
I always thought there was another way.

WE SHOULD HAVE TOLD YOU

That You Will Come to Feel That You Are Having Conversations With Someone Outside of Yourself # 10

My emotional clearing by way of bronchitis symptoms, resulted in me staying home from work for a few days each of the next several months. This kept me constantly behind at my job which I found to be extremely stressful. Which caused me to once again develop bronchitis symptoms. I felt like I was on a treadmill and I did not know how to get off. I decided that it was necessary for me to once again give Notice at my job.

Then I remembered that I had taken this Leap twice before and had not had things turn out as I had hoped they would. Was I really prepared to take that Leap again? Up came some fear, as I had not been at the job long enough to build up much in the way of savings. Still I did not feel that I could continue with the job. I told my company that I felt the need to give my 30 days Notice.

Immediately after reaching this decision, I went for a walk in the beautiful sunshine and I was So Happy, thinking that we should all be out in the sunshine doing what we wanted.

I seem to be on a rampage for freedom.

You are on the Freedom Train. You chose to get on that train when you decided to attend your son's wedding in Japan.

Did I make some commitment by agreeing to get on that train?

What has happened in your life since?

Since then, I quit my job, gave up my beautiful apartment and spent time in the homes of friends. Then I returned to my former job and got another apartment in my old neighborhood. Sometimes I wonder if I'm fooling myself that I'm progressing. And that I am actually stuck in the mud and continuously churning up the same old stuff.

WE SHOULD HAVE TOLD YOU

*That You Will Come to Feel That You Are Having
Conversations With Someone Outside of Yourself # 11*

Learning that a beginning agent was the only one available to take on my most difficult account, I offered to stay at the job for another month until other arrangements could be made. Following this additional month, my company proposed that I stay on at a reduced workload.

What is the part of me that could get excited about staying longer at my job?

Ask that Part of Yourself.

Hello Part. What Part of me are you?

The part that has frequently left without a proper goodbye.

Is there something that you would like to say?

I would like to say that I am frightened.

What are you frightened of?

I am frightened that once again you may ask me to pretend that I am big and strong and that I do not need anybody. I do need somebody. I need somebody to be there for me, somebody to tell me that I am doing a good job and that my efforts are appreciated. Someone to tell me that I am going to be OK and that I have what it takes to make my way.

WE SHOULD HAVE TOLD YOU

That Some of Your Beliefs Will Surprise You # 4

I decided to stay, and accept a reduced workload. Almost immediately after starting it, I began to experience discomfort about my situation. Was I OK with being seen as a person who was being given special consideration by getting to leave the office each day at 2 or 3 pm while my colleagues were there till 5 or 6 pm?

Was I OK with allowing my company to give me this special consideration because they thought I was physically weakened, when I knew that I had a choice? It was true that the stress of a full workload contributed to my physical symptoms of bronchitis. But I knew that these symptoms were because a large chunk of my emotional clearing involved my heart region and my breathing. So if I chose to ease back on my emotional clearing, I would be less susceptible to the bronchitis.

But I didn't want to ease back on this emotional clearing.

WE SHOULD HAVE TOLD YOU

That Some of Your Beliefs Will Surprise You # 5

The magnificent logistics of my reduced workload (lots of monies in exchange for few hours of work) was wonderful - and it was to be temporary. I immediately began wondering how I could possibly continue to have such working conditions. I realized that I wasn't certain that I could imagine creating the same again. Why was that? Even my rational mind said, why wouldn't your thinking be, that having done something once, you now have the template, so it would be easier to do it a second time? Why would one success not give me confidence and lead me to believe that I could do it again?

Do I believe there's only so much "good fortune" to go around and that I have had my share?

WE SHOULD HAVE TOLD YOU

That You Can Let Go of Your Beliefs # 2

Initially I thought that since my reduced workload required only 4-5 hours each day, why not go to the office first thing in the morning and get those hours out of the way?

But what I found was that once I had done my 4-5 hours at the office, my energy had changed and it was extremely difficult if not impossible for me to get back into the energy I had been in before I went to the office.

So I set up a schedule that on 3 of the 5 mornings, allowed me to sit with myself until 10 or 11 am before I pulled myself away to go to the office.

There went an Old Belief that I needed to get my chores done before I could justify having time off.

WE SHOULD HAVE TOLD YOU

That You Can Let Go of Your Beliefs # 3

I was sitting at home one morning thinking how I had a lot of work to do that day and that if I allowed myself to sit at home until 11 am then I should expect that things would be hectic when I went to work.

I held a Belief that if I goof off, I should expect to pay for it later.

I decided to consider a Belief that I could sit at home until 11 am and then go to the office and all would go smoothly and quickly.

And it did. There went another Belief.

WE SHOULD HAVE TOLD YOU

That You Will Begin to Feel a Connection With Objects # 1

I am a novice computer user - albeit an adventurous one. One morning as I was trying to unfreeze my computer, I found this thing that said "Defragment". Sensing that this would help, I started it up. I watched a little nervously as the program started. I may be adventurous - but not totally without fear.

A few minutes into the defragment, I realized that I was feeling an "energy exchange" with the computer, like we were going through something together - something that felt like a "birth". Part of me wanted to go and have my morning salt bath while another part felt that I would like to stay with my computer / friend who was going through this "birth".

After a few more minutes, I felt that it was appropriate for me to leave my computer / friend to defrag while I had my bath.

When I returned to my computer / friend, she was still defragging. I sat with "her" and tears came to my eyes - this is big for me as tears do not easily come to my eyes. I watched "her" process in fascination of "Oh look how one part seems to go ahead to clear the way for the part that is following."

And each time the program went back to pick up a little piece that seemed to have been flagged and left behind, more tears came to my eyes. I thought that's like what I seem to be doing. Each time I have some new learning, it's like I go back and heal little pieces from my past that were wounded because I didn't have the necessary learning at the time.

WE SHOULD HAVE TOLD YOU

That You Will Begin to Feel a Connection With Objects # 2

I discovered that "would-be thieves" had been in my car but had been unable to steal it. I was grateful that the car hadn't been stolen, grateful that the car would still start despite the gearbox having been tampered with and grateful that the registration papers had been left on the floor of the car.

But I was in shock at the condition of the car's interior and amazed at how much this affected me. Emotional reactions that started with how could I have been so Trusting and so Foolish as to leave my garage unlocked (though my car had been safe for 18 months in this unlocked garage). Then came guilt, as my car has served me well since I bought it several years earlier and it has been with me essentially through my whole Spiritual Journey. In fact it has in many ways been The Constant through my Journey. And during a few times of precarious financial choices, I had promised myself that I would not jeopardize losing it.

What to do next? The car's interior now felt to be "below the standard" of what I was allowing myself to believe that I deserved. I have not been very conscientious about cleaning the car's interior over the years and I have smoked in it, so this vandalism damage really tipped the scales.

And yet I was "responsible" for the car now being in this condition, I was the one who had left the garage unlocked. I fluctuated, should I investigate getting a new car at a time when I was unemployed? Would I even be able to buy a new car at this time?

One day I got the Knowing that I could drive to the GM dealer and arrange for a new car lease / purchase. That seemed to release my fear that maybe purchasing another car was not an option at this time. The next day my environmentalist side kicked in with: but the exterior of your car is fine, doesn't even look like an older car. So why would you consider replacing it?

I decided to go slowly, get the interior fixed, see how it looked and then decide. When I went to pick up my car after the repair, there it was sitting sparkling in the sunshine. "You've washed my car!" I exclaimed. "Yep, inside and out", said the man. And sure enough they had even shampooed the interior. I couldn't believe how excited I was to have my car back.

WE SHOULD HAVE TOLD YOU

That Sometimes Your Progress Will Be in Stages – Stage 1

The province where I live has House Lotteries offering lovely houses as prizes. I had come up with the idea that I would Put Out the Intention, that I would win one of these houses and develop a Retreat where others could join me in my Personal and Spiritual Growth. I had a really good feeling when I attended the viewing of a House that I thought would be suitable for a Retreat, so I bought a ticket. But I didn't win.

I had felt so strongly that I was going to win that house.

Yes, for a time it appeared that you would.

Then why didn't I?

There were several reasons. You were not really ready, a lesson for you in romantic relationships became available, and the floor plan was not right remember?

So have I been too demanding as to how the house should be?

Why do you tend to think that there was something wrong on your part when your requests are not answered in the way that you hoped? Do you think that it is possible that the timing was just not right? Or that you had other lessons to learn first?

WE SHOULD HAVE TOLD YOU

That Sometimes Your Progress Will Be in Stages – Stage 2

While waiting for another suitable house to become available, I had done a drawing that modified the floor plan of the first house. The floor plan of the second house was exactly as I had drawn, but the house was on a busy street. I came home somewhat frustrated after viewing this house.

So are you accepting the idea of continuing at your job as opposed to being at the Lottery House?

I hadn't expected an entrance on a busy street.

But you asked for it to be near a bus stop.

I was thinking maybe a block away.

Oh.

Stepping onto the deck was certainly wonderful.

That is in response to your desire to have a deck where people can sit and enjoy the ocean.

The floor plan is as I had drawn it.

So do you want the house?

Yes I would love it.

Yet you still have trouble believing it could be possible, do you not?

Yes I do. Why is that?

It is because you have a Belief that wonderful things do not happen for someone like you.

What does someone like me mean?

Someone who has never had these wonderful things.

Someone who has not worked hard enough.

Someone who is not deserving of them.

These are your beliefs. They are not ours.

WE SHOULD HAVE TOLD YOU

That Sometimes Your Progress Will Be in Stages – Stage 3

I received a brochure on another Lottery House that looked like it might be suitable for my Retreat House idea. The Lottery Foundation had purchased a waterfront estate, which had then been divided into 4 lots. I had visited the first house when it was built and had then wandered across the remaining land finding myself drawn to a spot at the water's edge.

As I stood on that spot with the wind in my face, I sensed that I had stood there before. It seemed to be some kind of a Power Spot for me as I felt both grounded and transported to another dimension at the same time. This Power Spot was on what I considered to be the most beautiful of the vacant lots. I had the feeling that my house would be built on that lot.

Well the house in the brochure was on the beautiful lot - but my Power Spot was actually on the neighboring lot whose view of the ocean was much less expansive.

Perhaps because the current house was on the lot with the view that I loved, I spent some time evaluating. One house had the view that I loved but did not contain my Power Spot. Also the house was not totally to my liking - it was stucco whereas I prefer wood, and it had black trim, which is possibly my least favorite color.

Is this about me needing to make a choice?

This is about issues and priorities. That was a valuable exercise that you did about comparing how you would feel if you were already sitting in your house on the ocean watching the rain - that you would be having the same thoughts and feelings as you are having now, just in a more glorious setting.

So it isn't about the House, it's about me?

Yes.

WE SHOULD HAVE TOLD YOU

That You Will Connect With the Energy of Other People # 1

I walked down to the beach for the Fireworks, found a tree facing the barge, and sat down to enjoy my hotdog. I finished the hotdog just as the fireworks began, so I stood up to lean my back against the tree.

As I was tossing my napkin into the garbage bin, I noticed a man leaning against the side of "my" tree. Thinking that I recognized him, I turned in the twilight for a closer look. Nope, not the guy I thought. But my mind registered that he was a handsome hunk of a male.

As the fireworks progressed, I became very aware of the energy of this hunk beside me (well on the side of my tree). As I continued to watch the fireworks, I could feel the hunk's energy and mine meet and blend in a very balancing way. At one point, it felt like the most natural thing to do, would be to reach out for his hand. Amazing!

I considered that when the fireworks were over, I might tell him how much I had enjoyed his energy, that he had lovely energy - whatever. Then I decided, No, if I freak him out, I will spoil this wonderful sensation that I am having and which I am going to take home with me. So that's what I did.

WE SHOULD HAVE TOLD YOU

That You Will Connect With the Energy of Other People # 2

A new member joined a Discussion Group that I attend. As this new member shared some of her life experiences to date, I was thinking how she seemed intelligent, optimistic, had led a most interesting life, and had had some amazing insights. As I was walking home, I asked why my mind was "abuzz". The answer I got was "from listening to all of that woman's 'facts'." Hmmm.

Then I noticed that my chest was tight, which for me, usually indicates the presence of "anger energy". So, I walked and I Breathed, and yet I couldn't connect with anything that I was angry about.

Then one comment of the woman's "sharing" came to my mind, and I thought, she's the one who is angry, and I have picked up this "angry energy" from her.

WE SHOULD HAVE TOLD YOU

That You Will Connect With the Energy of Other People # 3

As it was a very warm summer day I wandered out, picked up a falafel wrap and headed to the beach where I sat on a bench. As I began opening my falafel, I noticed that a man seated nearby had turned to stare at me. I could "feel" that he wanted my food. I found myself resenting that he was interfering with my enjoyment.

Then my old tapes started playing: "maybe I'll eat half and then give him the rest, maybe I'll give him $5 so he can buy something for himself". Then I thought, but this feeling isn't coming from my core, I feel that I'm reacting to energy that he's putting out.

As I had this realization, I could feel my energy somewhat congealing into a ball and forming a bit of a shield between the man and me. My energy seemed to do this on its own. I had the thought that my energy was choosing to keep itself "intact".

At this point the man got restless, stood up, stretched, walked about and then laid on the grass directly in front of me - and now closer to me than he had been when sitting on the bench. Even though he was lying on his back and facing away from me, I was very aware of his energy - and it was on my food.

After lying on the ground for a few minutes, the man got up and came to sit behind me on the bench. I didn't turn around to see how close he was, but my energy body must have thought he was really close, as I felt it develop a thicker wall between us.

After a few more minutes, having eaten all of my Falafel, I decided to leave - without looking back. As I walked away my mind searched, asking "Have you no compassion, do you not think it would have been loving to share? " But another part of me said, this was about more than compassion or being loving. This was about learning to contain your energy and to choose with whom you are going to share it.

WE SHOULD HAVE TOLD YOU

That There Will Be Times When You Will Just Be in the Flow

I decided to walk to the neighborhood London Drugs for some items. As I was preparing to leave my apt, I saw some "2 for 1" coupons from McDonalds which is next door to London Drugs. I don't think I can remember the last time I was in a McDonald's, yet I felt nudged to slip these coupons into my pocket. I then found myself walking directly to McDonalds and ordering 2 Big Mac dinners to go.

I was waiting for the dinners to be delivered to me, and asking myself, what was I going to do with 2 McDonald dinners, when my bag of food arrived. As I turned around with the bag of food in my hand, one of the small tables emptied, so I went and sat down and began opening the bag of food. As I did so, I became aware of a man with the appearance of a homeless or street person sitting beside me, nursing a coffee.

I heard myself asking him if he had had his dinner. He said no, he hadn't. So I said, well now I know why I ordered 2 dinners, and I set out a dinner for each of us. Once our dinners were set out, we each read our paper and ate our dinner with no more interaction with each other.

As I was leaving, the man said Thank You and gave me the most grateful smile. I walked away thinking of the perfection, that he was there at that time, that I ordered 2 dinners, that the table beside him was the one that became available etc.

I also thought of the flip side, of him sitting there hungry, smelling the food, and then being presented with a dinner. And I thought of how I want to remember this, at times when I'm sitting somewhere, wondering how I am going to receive something that I would like to have. That maybe at that very moment, there is someone walking towards me with the very piece that I am missing.

WE SHOULD HAVE TOLD YOU

That Other People Have Their Own Reality

My son emails about his new baby, his first child. He's so excited, can't believe he's actually a dad etc.

At one point, he says he thinks the baby looks like him. I look at the picture he has emailed of the baby and I think, does she? I totally forget, that I have never been "good" at seeing who babies look like. So I ask, if his wife agrees. He answers that everyone agrees. Do I stop then? No, I write back, well I can see yes to the forehead and the eyes, don't know about the lower face.

Later, I'm walking along and I think, what was that about? What came to me, was that it was about insecurity on my part. Thoughts of what kind of mother can't tell whether this baby looks like her son did when he was a baby

After receiving the next batch of pictures I sent an email that said, "Have I mentioned that your daughter grows more beautiful in each picture, and since she looks like her dad, she will continue to do so?"

And you know what? The guy stepped right back onto his old Joyful Papa path. It was like my previous comments had been erased from his Reality.

WE SHOULD HAVE TOLD YOU

That Some Experiences Will Seem Weird Even to You # 2

The manager of the apartment building where I live was teasing me, because I usually seem to vacuum at the same time as she is vacuuming in the hall outside my door. She said to me "You're not vacuuming?" I looked around and said "No my place is clean."

Then in my sleep I dreamed that I was in an apartment where there were Dust Bunnies all over the place - I mean there were Dust Bunnies on the walls!

And when I woke this morning there were so many Dust Bunnies in my apt. I couldn't believe it. None on the walls granted - but in several places on the floor. And less than 24 hours after it had been Clean!

I guess I'm wondering if the Dust Bunnies followed me home.

WE SHOULD HAVE TOLD YOU

That Your Body Will Give You Messages

The government had decided that it was necessary to License we Property Agents. My colleagues and I were informed that our company had registered us for a study seminar that was scheduled for a Saturday, a treasured day to myself for me. I felt strongly, that I did not want to attend.

Oh what turmoil I allowed myself to experience. And what fears - all the way to "Was I prepared to jeopardize my job?" My cells screamed "No, we won't go". My rational mind said, "It's only one day, it's a requirement of licensing for your job, you will have to do it sooner or later". But, "NO, we won't go!" Then I "accidentally" discovered that the seminar would also be offered on the following Tuesday. I decided that I would attend then.

On the Monday following the Saturday seminar, I arrived at my office to learn that when my colleagues arrived at the seminar, they had learned that attending the seminar was not in fact a requirement of our licensing. I felt so happy and so grateful that I had listened to my screaming cells and stayed home.

WE SHOULD HAVE TOLD YOU

That You Can Communicate With Your Body

My body is carrying a large amount of flesh on my mid torso. Do I need to be concerned about that?

Ask your Body.

Body, do I need to be concerned?

Well, you could feed me a little less – as long as I still know that you love me.

And how could I let you know that?

Well, you could talk to me and touch me – the same way that you show others that you love them.

OK. What would you like to talk about?

I would like you to thank me for all that I have done for you. I am the one that helped you win glory as an athlete, the one who bore your children, the one who has given you hours of delight in the bedroom and on the dance floor.

Yes, you are. Thank You.

And I have seldom been ill except for that Breathing issue, which was a reflection of Emotional Clearing and nothing to do with me except that I was working with you to facilitate that clearing.

WE SHOULD HAVE TOLD YOU

That Your Body Holds Memories # 2

Regarding my increased body size, I hear words like self-important, puffing oneself up, being seen. What are these phrases about?

They are about how you see yourself. Part of you senses that you are becoming big and powerful. You have spent many Lifetimes as a Warrior when size and strength were important. You have memories of a need to protect yourself knowing that you may face danger. You can now release those memories. Let them go, knowing that you no longer require bulk and strength. You now require heart strength and courage.

I had a vision of strings going out from the top of my heart. Are those strings attached to something?

Yes. They are attached to others and to expectations.

So, do I now detach those strings?

Yes. Yes. Yes.

I feel loss and then strength rushing in at the same time.

Yes because now you are containing the energy that is being sent to you. You are temporarily holding enough energy to seal the openings to those old strings that were attached to your heart.

WE SHOULD HAVE TOLD YOU

That You Should Ask For Exactly What You Want # 1

A couple of weeks after my daughter's graduation, her dad, who lives in another province, forwarded some pictures by computer adding that if I wanted more pictures to let him know. I answered jokingly that I would like a picture of me thinner and with longer hair.

A few days later in the mail I received copies of the computer pictures. Along with the pictures there was a newspaper clipping of a woman, slimmer than me and with hair longer than mine - and who had my name. Now I'm thinking, why didn't I add more items to my request list?

Also because my request manifested I've been sitting with "the process" - trying to remember the feeling state I was in, when I made my request. I had looked at the pictures on the computer and had thoughts of me being larger and with shorter hair than I like.

And then I had let those thoughts go, I guess deciding that things were as they were, there was nothing I could do about it now, and maybe that it really wasn't that important to me, especially in light of all the other wonderful things that surrounded the graduation event.

So when the suggestion of other pictures came up, the words came out of my mouth without emotion attached - yet they also contained my Truth - I would have liked to be thinner with longer hair, but was not going to beat myself up, or feel that I needed to do anything about it. And of course, because it was just a joke, I never thought of it again. And then it happened.

Or maybe and so it happened.

WE SHOULD HAVE TOLD YOU

That You Should Ask For Exactly What You Want # 2

I'm remembering a time when I had found myself in a position where I needed to find both a place to live and a way to pay for it immediately. Within a week I found myself in a house-sitting situation and with a well paying job for which I was marginally qualified.

At the time I was amazed and grateful for what seemed to be miracles. But I have sometimes looked back and wondered what may have happened, had I not been so locked into the Belief that having a job was the only way that my needs could be met. I did get what I asked for - a place to live and a way to pay for it.

But now I wonder what might have happened, if I had stated my Real Truth, which was that I wanted to continue my unstructured life and to have my bills taken care of.

WE SHOULD HAVE TOLD YOU

That Sometimes Current Situations Will Trigger Old Memories

I learned that two of my colleagues had given Notice to leave the job. I anticipated a "we'd like you to take on more accounts" talk with the VP in the next few days. I did not want to take on more accounts but I wondered why I was dreading the discussion that I sensed would be necessary for me to achieve this.

Up came the memory of a Journey from my Native American Teachings classes:

I heard "there's more that you're not telling". I felt that there was something that I was refusing to admit that I knew, maybe even something that I wasn't supposed to know and that some authority figure wanted me to tell or to admit. I was afraid that I might divulge this information.

As I asked myself what I thought this could be about, I felt pressure in my throat, which tightened until I felt like I was being "choked". Asking myself who would be choking me, I had a vision of a "hanging knot" around my throat. There was a 6-8 inch extension of rope beyond the knot though I didn't have a sense that the knot was attached to anything.

Then I had a sense of asking myself do you think you've been hanged? I answered that yes, I think so. At this point my neck got really tight. I sensed both because the rope got tighter and because I got very afraid. I asked myself if I could release my fear of death. I was able to answer yes and the pressure on my neck decreased.

Next I sensed sadness, thinking of loved ones who would be grieving my death. I asked, can I release this sadness? After a brief time, I was able to answer yes. Then I asked about the people who were instrumental in me being hanged – could I forgive them? I answered yes.

All of these answers came quite quickly.

Suddenly there came a quite loud question of "why are you being hanged"? I didn't come up with a definite answer. I heard "did you do something to bring this upon yourself"? Still no answer, but I think a growing sense that I wasn't totally innocent. Then I heard "do you feel guilty, are you sorry for what you have done"? The guilt was heavy, thick and cold and didn't release.

So maybe my dread of the anticipated talk with the VP has to do with a memory of having to speak to an authority figure.

WE SHOULD HAVE TOLD YOU

That There Will Be Times When You Will Be Protected

I had rather forgotten about the whole issue of a possible talk with the VP as my son was visiting and we were doing family stuff. My son left one morning and that evening I remembered the work thing and I thought, "Hey, I must have escaped that ordeal". Not so! The next morning I got the "I need to see you for a few minutes" email from the VP.

Since the request was by email, I decided to take a smoke break before I responded. I was amazed at the feelings that came up during this smoke break. I don't want to do more accounts. Well, maybe I could do this much more. Maybe I could trade one of my smaller accounts for a larger one, etc. etc.

I even saw myself start the tape that said, "don't you dare change things, I want things to stay just the way they are, until I have manifested what I really want".

And then I remembered, that I had been seeing my job as temporary and wondering why "what I really want" had not been manifesting. Aha! - "what I really want" has not been manifesting because I have been holding onto "things staying just the way they are until...."

This Aha threw me into total confusion. I can't remember the last time I was so unbalanced.

But Someone accompanied me to that talk because I ended up with things staying the same. And not by my own doing. I wasn't capable of negotiating. At one point I even said to the VP, "I don't even know what I want".

So, maybe the "good news" from this is that we are somehow "protected" and almost can't screw up.

WE SHOULD HAVE TOLD YOU

That You Really Do Know a Lot

I was to write a Licensing exam, required to allow me to continue with my current career, should I choose. The "problem" was that I just did not feel like studying. I wondered if I was maybe removing a safety net - that if I failed the exam, I would not be able to return to my current career.

My heart reminded me that I did not want to continue with that line of work anyway. My mind said that it would be a good idea to get licensed "just in case".

The day before the exam, I opened the study text, and it was like my vision went right through the print, the words didn't even register. And the feeling of "Not Wanting To" came over me really strongly and it was like I remembered so many times, that I had made myself do something that I didn't want to do. And I put the study text away.

After that, I felt calm - like something had been decided and everything would be OK - either I would pass the exam or it wouldn't matter.

I'd be lying if I didn't admit to having a few anxious moments before I went to sleep that night. The idea that I might wake in terror in the wee hours and do some frantic last minute "cramming" felt like a possibility.

WE SHOULD HAVE TOLD YOU

*That You Will Come to Feel That You Are Having
Conversations With Someone Outside of Yourself # 12*

What's up with me and this exam that I'm writing today?

You are releasing a control that says that writing this exam is necessary for you or for anyone. What does the exam prove for either those who choose to continue with this work or for you who are choosing not to continue?

Yet I sense to write the exam, not to just sit home.

Yes because by writing the exam you will learn something - possibly that you can pass the exam without studying, possibly that the material is totally irrelevant, possibly that you can now play with something that others take so seriously.

Following this conversation I called a cab to take me to the building where I was to write the exam, as I didn't feel sufficiently grounded to deal with looking for parking, etc.

Once in the exam room, I read through the exam and I had the thought that I knew "about 80%" of the material. So I wrote in my answers, handed in the papers and left the room in a bit of a daze, like I couldn't believe what I had just done.

A few days later I opened my mailbox to see that the exam results had arrived. I sat for a bit before opening the envelope asking myself what I waned the results to say.

When I reached the point where I was OK either way pass or fail, I opened the envelope. I had passed. And guess what my score was? 78%.

Now, it's true that this was not an unknown field for me. I had been working in it for 6 years. Still, I find it significant that I had known that I knew "about 80%" and I scored 78%.

We really do know a lot.

WE SHOULD HAVE TOLD YOU

That You Will Begin Getting Messages in Your Dreams # 1

In a dream I was asleep on a mattress on the floor of my office building and I became aware that there was a rat in the room with me. Then it was like the rat had suctioned onto my blanket and the rat was shaking itself furiously. I sensed danger but I was so deeply asleep, that I couldn't pull myself out of my sleep to take any action except to pull the blanket over my head.

Upon waking I looked at my present home and work environments and asked myself why am I continuing to work at a job that does not make my heart sing?

Are you Staying or are you Going?

Is that question about more than my job? It feels like I am being asked if I really want to stay on Earth. There were some moments last week when I wasn't certain that I could stay or that I wanted to stay.

When you have the thought of how easy it would have been to choose to leave, it is actually a confirmation that you have reaffirmed your decision to stay.

WE SHOULD HAVE TOLD YOU

That You Will Begin Getting Messages in Your Dreams # 2

In another dream I got up from the desk in my office and went into the hallway. The hallway had changed and now had a door between my office and the neighboring office and my office was now part of offices belonging to a different company. I felt in No Man's Land between my old company and this new company.

Following this dream I began noticing a new reaction on my part to phone calls from clients. The reaction was that many times I didn't seem to respond, to the point where the client must have wondered if I was actually still present. It didn't necessarily feel like withdrawal or avoidance in the old sense, just a blankness.

Like one client did the intimidating thing - no response from me just a blank. Another client did the poor me why is no-one helping me thing - no response from me just a blank. It's not that I felt anger or fear in response to the intimidating client, or Oh Please in response to the poor me client, it's like part of my mind was saying this has nothing to do with us. Maybe, it's like the song "I'm Already Gone."

WE SHOULD HAVE TOLD YOU

That You Will Begin to Trust Synchronicity # 3

Not long after having these dreams and my new reaction to clients, a series of events happened or didn't happen, that resulted in my company taking me off my largest account (which I have been wanting for months) and the VP saying that they didn't really have another "good" account to offer me at the moment.

So I said, maybe this can work for each of us, as I have been wanting some time off. The VP and I discussed the status of my other accounts, and agreed that I would begin a Leave of Absence in a month.

It looks like I'm getting what I asked for and it terrifies me.

It usually does terrify.

And why is that, why does it terrify me to feel that I'm getting what I want – or that I think I want?

It has to do with what you want being closer, not so far away. This forces you to accept the reality and to release the longing. There is comfort and familiarity in longing, like a mental "if only" that you can hold onto.

WE SHOULD HAVE TOLD YOU

That Sometimes It Will Feel Like You Are Going in Circles # 2

I have left jobs before for extended periods of time hoping to find my "passion" only to always return to jobs that "pay the bills"– so I have a memory of failure. One day I thought how previously, I had tended to stay focused on work until I quit and then once I was unemployed, I would start focusing on my unemployed state with its associated pressures and fears

This time I thought, why don't you fast-forward this movie you've been to before and pretend that you're already unemployed. That way you can experience the pressures and the fears while you also have the luxury and comfort of a pay check.

And you know, it worked. For 24 hours I was in absolute terror.

Thank You to the part of me that during this time, reminded me of previous times of turmoil when I have survived.

WE SHOULD HAVE TOLD YOU

That When You Follow Your Heart You Cannot Fail

I'm beginning to see that when I felt like I was on a treadmill and needing to give Notice at work, I followed my heart and gave Notice. I later extended that Notice to prevent a colleague from getting a tough account which led to me getting an offer of part time work. One year later I felt to not go to a seminar, and it turned out that the seminar was not compulsory. All is well always, it is impossible for us to fail, so we should choose what we want most.

In the bath I had the realization that things that are meant for me are and have been looking for me. I cried a little thinking but if they've been looking for me why have I felt so alone? Why didn't I know that they were looking for me?

I heard it was a timing thing.

Then I explored how do I feel now that I know that these things are looking for me just as I have been looking for them? I felt maybe more sadness than relief, even though I know that if I'm looking for them and they're looking for me, it is inevitable that we find each other.

WE SHOULD HAVE TOLD YOU

*That Things Feel More Difficult When the Finish Line
Is in Sight*

I sense that I'm at a really major point in my learning curve and I am about to make a quantum leap. Like bits and pieces of my puzzle are falling into place. Then I thought that maybe leaving my job is symbolically about finishing this Journey I've been on. The Finish Line is in sight, I am tired, I want to rest, to be comforted, and to be supported.

All of you, now that you can see the Finish Line, want to cross that line and bask in the glory. That will come. There's just a bit more work to be done before the basking. It's actually harder now that the Finish Line is in sight. Do not go backwards.

Remember that you are never alone, that you are loved, and that you will be cared for.

Is cared for the same as provided for?

You will provide for yourself with our assistance.

And who are you who will be assisting me?

We are your Angelic Team, those who have known you in other lifetimes and in other Realities. We come here now to assist you as you take this very important next step, important both in your own development and in the development of Humanity. We Thank You for your Agreement to take this step and for the courage that you show by doing so.

We have All of Us awaited and hoped for this next step for eons of time. And we are grateful and excited that it has now arrived. It is like a Birth. The gestation period has been long and at times arduous. At times we wondered if Indeed there would ever Be Completion and Fruition.

Now the time is upon us.

CROSSOVER TIME

Seeking, searching, looking for a clue
What to think? What to do?
Embracing the new, leaving the old behind
Relax, breathe deeply; it's Crossover Time

Your life's a mess, you're totally confused
You've lost your job, you've been abused
You're hurt, you're angry, afraid you might die
Relax, breathe deeply; it's Crossover Time

You rant, you rave, you rail, you cry
Try as you might, you can't understand why
None of the old formulas seem to be working
Relax, breathe deeply; it's Crossover Time

Cross over to what you ask through the pain
Why shouldn't I expect just more of the same?
Because the world is changing; that's the reason why
Relax, breathe deeply; it's Crossover Time

Time to question, time to trust
What is a desire, what is a must
The musts have to go so the desires can flow4
Relax, breather deeply; it's Crossover Time.

About the Author...

Sharon Clark Rowlands was born and raised on Prince Edward Island, Canada. After graduating from the University of New Brunswick, she married and made her way to Canada's west coast. There then followed years as a parent with jobs in schoolteaching and sales and marketing, interspersed with the pursuit of personal growth and metaphysical studies and practices. In 2008, she was inspired to combine excerpts from her many years of Journal writing and examples of her personal experiences into her first manuscript, **Oh, We Should Have Told You.**